Moorings

Carolyn Masel

Moorings

Acknowledgments

Some of these poems have been published in the following journals and anthologies:
Scripsi, *The Circle* (University of Toronto School of Graduate English), *The Exhibition Room* (University of Essex Literature Department), *Assemblage: New International Writing* (University of Essex), *Eureka Street*, *Wild* (Ginninderra Press).

To Bob,
Jon, Mim and Rebecca,

and to Jenny, Caro and Penelope,
who waited even longer,

with love and gratitude

Moorings
ISBN 978 1 76041 720 8
Copyright © text Carolyn Masel 2019
Cover design by Jon DiNapoli, with elements from a photograph by Julien Leyre at australianaesthetics.wordpress.com/trams

First published 2019 by
GINNINDERRA PRESS
PO Box 3461 Port Adelaide 5015 Australia
www.ginninderrapress.com.au

Contents

Returns	7
In Spaces Between	9
Ours are the daydream streets	10
Spring in Melbourne With Doves	11
Students	13
Poem for Vin	14
Aerial Footage	15
Coventry Carol	17
Like a kaleidoscope on a timer	19
You hope by blanking them out	21
Early Spring in Middle Earth	22
In Fitzroy Gardens	24
Bespoke	26
Tree Pose	27
Called to Account	28
Lifecraft	29
To Bec in France	30
Fleurs du Mal	31
Not Invisible, Alas	34
Two Pastorals	35
Shepherd	37
So	38
No Possums	39
Portrait of a Religious Man	40
After Long Darkness	41
Aphasia, Exile, Outlawry	42
Exile	45
Double Vision	47
Summer Song, Toronto	50

From a Tall Building in Toronto	51
Doubt	53
Letter in December	54
London	56
Morning Song	58
After the Great Storm	59
Colchester, a walking song	60
Radio Drama	62
In Memoriam Francis Barker	63
Poem in April	64
Tatton Park	65
Song for Esther	66
Notes from the First Gulf War	67

Moorings 71

Moonrise (a fragment)	73
The house was called The Moorings	74
This is a false memory	77
Rejection	78
Poem for Caro	79
Nocturne	81
Sans Bulot	82
Mother	83
Task (Visiting Grandpa)	84
Intimations	86
Four a.m.	87

Returns

In Spaces Between

for Jack Charles

She sits meekly in the back,
ankles crossed,
hands clasped,
defying interference.

She has only to look out
to ride the cowcatcher
in front of the tram,
then the footboard, then

grab the passing car-door handle
with three fingers, and,
feet first, float her body
straight up like a kite

or spring from roof to roof
across the crumbling city,
hiding behind awnings,
sleeping by train lines,

quiet as dirt,
safe from all lassoing eyes –
they've not even caught a glimpse of her,
free as a cartwheeling windblown seed.

Ours are the daydream streets

Ours are the daydream streets
you drive past, humming –
little plots, whose houses
don't interrupt
with fashionable
features or picturesque
plantings

Our hill
drops down
like a bridge in a dream,
the footpath
        click-clacks
                down;
Then follow your nose to the river
unmoving, tidal, brown –
cold   wind
        riffling the shine

Look across:
        apartment blocks
        church spires
        piercing skies
        a city's clumped silhouette

Spring in Melbourne With Doves

Like parents we wait
while the season does its awkward flip,
heads bent in the gale driving cloud
shadows across the page
– as if we needed another prophecy.

Wind tires in the roof vents.
A cube of space forms round us, and comforting sounds.
Our crotchety dogs resume their dialogue
with distant quavers

                demisemiquavers
      Till a helicopter,
      hummingbird from hell,
      burrs all thought,
            and ratchets up and away

leaving doves' mad
repetitious purring

New research shows city birds call louder.
Today they're the only thing that doesn't
sound like something else you can't escape.

Ipse. Same. The selfsame birds
telling all their lives in that same sound,
as though condemned to the residue of speech.

Wait.
      Remember Robert Duncan –
how, when he learned of the stroke that killed the words
in H.D., beloved poet mentor,
he turned to the ur-language of doves, hearing
there the originary Word.

Something's aflutter. Dog among the pigeons?
      What you doin' with that metaphor?
      Taboo, treif, *two thousand years!*
      Who do you think you are? Paul Simon?
And on and on, patrolling the dream ground.

Jokes aside, I'd give a bucket of dreams
for a minute with the minstrel of all the world.
He's pulled out the knife that divides us
and mines for song in the site of the wound.
Hallelujah! Good for him!
So far, I feel compelled to leave it in.

It's not that you could undo understanding
a style of understanding. It's what you say.
As collared doves should not be here but are –
invaders, refugees or immigrants
or offspring of same,
conceived in St Petersburg, born in Bendigo.
Glad to be here. Bobbing their heads, side

by bright-eyed side, out there on the bricks,
despite their interminable double-cadenced cry,
there's every sign they're making sense of it all.

Students

Not even young creatures. Just
spirits barely housed,
                        beguiled
into this accommodation.

How is it with them?
        Some return a blank gaze.
        Some lower lids, consulting.
        Some let in sunlight
        through the tops of their heads –

        Those are the ones.

Poem for Vin

in memory of Vincent Buckley

It is night. I am reading Charles Wright's
Chicamauga, how he yearns
for silence undisturbed by word
or desire: to fade without a break
into trees and grass
as the landscape itself fades
in waning light.
I know this. I recall
standing in a field in Suffolk just after you died,
with each tree, each blanched tussock
perfectly resigned to earth, asking nothing.
I stood a long time
in that wintry Eden,
unconvinced, for once, of death's finality…
Now I read on, thinking,
God, you would love this stuff –

Aerial Footage

homage to Michel de Certeau

A French philosopher went up the Tower
to spurn the matchless view. In principle.
New York City sparkled at his feet.

How to convince them of their value down there:
the spontaneity of life on the street –
its chaos, brio, democratic lack

of vista… Whereas up here, perilous-
ly close to the eyeball of God
(that insatiable, designing orb),

you could forget it all, and just hang
like a planet, while the lights went out…
He looked at the moon. It wasn't having any;

never one for rancour, or anything much,
serene or lobotomised, presiding
over everything with an equal mind:

a vacant city sailing in the void…
a brave philosopher's last seminar…
another crumpled Tower for the set…

and another. Eyes fill with horror
at the moon-cold screen, compelled
by repetitions of the spectacle.

Now we're only given distance shots.
Jumping, screaming, drowning strictly forbidden,
all cities, all countries, unreal –

if we believed the footage. Well, we don't.
Our life-and-death as citizens depends
on peopling empty landscapes, seeing ghosts,

rebuilding dwellings, with gardens, pets and food
and drink, in the teeth of the mindless grin of the moon.
The world's a jewel in space, but nobody's fooled.

Coventry Carol

for Roger Hillman

A banksia flower spike
wobbling on a spindle
holes cut in wood
to let out sound,
organ pipes or little beaks,
animal mouths
open and close like speaking wounds
as song unwinds

The body is weeping:
milk and tears and blood
make no sound,
numb mothers in a line:
tongues of stone

*

Hardly known at school
lightly, sure-footed
she crossed into the light

My daughter wept
her young face
shocked by hot tears

We can't explain so
many or stop them
jumping under
or out of –
blessed are the meek
for they find the violent Absolute…

Games where you can't
die or (only scroll
down)
are virtually
remembered forever –
Blessed are the pure in spirit
for they shall act authentically,
blessed are those who weep by the wall…

*

Years ago, in Withington
Cemetery, late for a service,
searching a cloverleaf asphalt path:
in each little clearing
six or seven young shocked burning –
distraught mascara –
no one over twenty…

*

This week we're teaching lullabies;
I can't find the old tune
for Mother Courage's song to Kattrin –
all day it sings inside me,
bye bye lully lullay

Like a kaleidoscope on a timer

Like a kaleidoscope on a timer
click look
        click click look
                click click yeah look
                it's staring you in the
                face looking back at you

and there you are again
        in a different town
your same ears going hot and cold
though thankfully you look like stupid stone –
        you can count on it

Re-run those eyes performing directness
that speech pitched to someone just behind you…
who knows how many know
        how foolish you are
        playing the fools' fool
            like a child in mud

It sweeps over you
from left to right like a sentence – it's
judgement, it's
whatever you should have he will have
she's already they were waiting for you to
or rather they weren't

and if it hurts you've only not careful
what do you expect by now can we not
about this please can we not

later

                       expert

                                            cauterise

When it stops that last
translucent ice-chip
you call the moon
drops like a blade

You hope by blanking them out

You hope by blanking them out
                         they'll go away
you've got good at it
             no edges show
but today they flipped their square signs round
to show designer faces
                 so
                               trained

a casual cull's impersonal as sport
and just as much a pleasure

Early Spring in Middle Earth

In my dream in the Mediterranean
it is spring, season of mermaids –
and there they are, bodies outstretched
just above the seabed.
she spreads her fin,
        translucent, like cicadas' wings,
                sending the ripple of an underwater breeze
                        to the child on the sand by her side.
Their hair is dark.
        She knows what to do.
                You cannot hear her song.

Materials change: now fluoro and black
chunks of sea serpent curve round a shoreline
approached by a lifeboat
in fog thick as paint.
Charon steers deftly behind.

Two figures wade out before the boat can land:
a child is lifted
                over the water
                        to waiting arms.

You too dream of taking them in,
as if your arms were their safest home –
but second-guessing trips you: is it
only the romance of gestures?
only children you could carry yourself?
No. It is not
Yin spreading cloud across the ocean,
this urge to embrace, enfold,
and not like hungry Whitman, death
lapping at his heels, or Yeats, magus-eyed,
staring at the park where Lady Gregory's
son once gazed and sketched the view.
It is required to harbour them, and if
the world seems too harsh for our watery eyes,
our tears must wear it away. Alas!
we have already reached Act V
where Lear can only repeat one word
while we press our lips in silence
       and the soldier carrying the child up the beach
           averts his face.

In Fitzroy Gardens

You sit down beside
the tree with delicate leaves
like green eyelashes
and round pine cones: little worlds…
Where would this one be at home?

Its bright breath calms you
It flourishes here without
knowing its own name –
To live without words like that
To be left alone to be…

You're dreaming again.
Rouse yourself, square your shoulders.
Communication,
a condition of being
human, takes superhuman

effort, it seems. So
start making the hard, strange sounds
in this stiff new tongue,
that your children may not know
such bitter-eyed frustration.

Let necessity
carve out new, responsive selves
who know the difference
between being emptied out
and a rare moment of poise –

such as this green cone's
unlikely geometry,
this deep wordless peace,
in a park of Australian
monsters with clattering leaves —

All the trees are loud.
Sound is breaking in. Stories.
Why is that ogre
singing as he strolls along?
Who are those whining creatures

under that dark tree
straight out of a mountain cave?
And who's sitting here
on the verge of asking, who
are all those other people

dotted evenly
as on a tram at midday —
each choosing a tree,
choosing words, the leaves spread out
like clouds in a common sky?

Bespoke

Elle's knitting a scarf.
She brings it to Poetry.
Everyone is calmed.

Put your knitting down.
We want to wear poetry
spun in your warm voice.

Tree Pose

The gum tree is still as a yogi
but mad with currawongs.
REALLY? Really? Really? Really?
They fly away in clumps
and back again,
arcing like thoughts between dendrites:
an utterly new idea.
Really? Really? Really?
The tree is having a brainwave.

Called to Account

I like Miss Bean
for singing the hymns out gladly,
for being robust
as a cup of tea.

You're looking pale, she says,
and I wonder what on earth?
(I've always been pale,
like her dresses are blue.)

It's Maths, I venture,
but could I ever say
how hard it is to express
x in relation to y

when x was minus y
so long ago
there's zero to add
as far as I'm concerned?

The numbers are not greater or smaller than.
They have to stand by themselves.
Like that one over there
at the edge of the schoolyard

watching the big kids
on pogo sticks and cable reels
while you look on
from the school's high office.

Lifecraft

for Jen Couch

In the absence of a champion
you build from skerricks:
the woman who called you *Ducks*…
the one who said *Darling*…
the one who said *Darling* by mistake…
flecks of colour from a mouthful of wine

every tiny element
strung on memory's banner
in the highest place
between you and your sky

These, you say, *are the ones.*
And thanks. It is enough.

Later the champions come –
the one who sings up the stars
the one who opens the poem of life
the one who waits to retrieve you from hell

Beloved voices,
whom to recollect is calm,
be near me, sound in my throat and chest.
Gentle my hand.

To Bec in France

All along the freeway
trees lean one way.
They look broken-hearted,
shrivelled with loss.

Inside, it's as if
a little cat has run away.
Her bell don't ring.
Our days stretch out.

Meaning leaches out of
words I didn't say:
that thing in your room was a locust
you might not now recall.

Some were found on the tennis courts –
Nadal was not amused.
His injuries are mending.
You always liked single combat.

It's too hot to sleep.
I think of you in a field of snow,
bright and cold,
laughing at everything.

Fleurs du Mal

(or Mrs Horner Shows Concern About the Fruit)

In vestigial darkness you might glimpse
men purposeful as spiders
going through abandoned streets.
Or hear, spliced into a dream,
two car doors slam, the car take off,
and no word said.
Far off glass breaks, gears shift
up, and you're caught
in the grittiest real,
the glitch between day and night,
with tear ducts frozen and newspapers poised
to deliver the latest acts.
                              While in their room
the kids are given to sleep,
flopped like sausages or clowns,
all smooth skin and long eyelashes.
Here in this setting for absent selves,
the question's not of love but simply care.
How could these get from here
to there?

Early traumas last, the experts say –
apparently they know whose cuts hurt most –
but memory can resemble an old wound
that presages damp days or like a sharp
new line make one gasp again.

What violence do they endure who
with nightmare slowness flee a wolfish past?
And are theirs unexamined lives who have
attained the modern armour-plated dream?

Some, capable of anything,
must have cauterised their memory,
sealed off all pain but, with that, pleasure too.
No echoes trouble them, or shining quiet,
no fear of losing half-recalled
breath warming their smaller hands
that had no use for printless gloves,
a fingertip lifting a strand of hair off the face
whose planes of stone now bar all touch.

We grow dull with forgetting until it's too late:
we're in love with the blankness that damns us,
that watches with indifference while we die.

Unless, unbidden, memory unfurls,
slowly at first, its hidden loops
of story, voices, floating free –
suspended, bending, bunching, stretched,
like shapes ink makes released in water,
the words love writes on thirsty skin.

Felt again, that touch
is not to be gainsaid,
compels us to gentle our hands, supports us
in a world grown lavish with praise –

as if the air itself remembered our names;

our voices move through it like replies.

Not Invisible, Alas

Late middle-age:
qualification and second-guessing –
at least two competing
remarks, world views, women, who cares!
Stick to the non-risqué one, thank you…

lest you recall
the day of trumpeting protest
closing your eyes won't make go away,
so you have to work out, shuteye,
which bit of objectionable
flesh must be visible

while noting that trumpet squeal of disgust
is actually at least two notes –
not,
emphatically not, the Buddhist monks'
rumbling ground bass and harmonics

Two Pastorals

I

In the absence of parkland –
trees, vistas, statues, water,
maintained by invisibles paid by same,
where you could walk and talk by yourself,
serious as the Queen –

you would settle for a beach-house
within sound of wave-break and suck
of the outgoing tide,
on sand pitted with morning rain,
drenched in eucalyptus

But the woman who disappeared from Lorne
after messaging goodnight
to family at the life saving carnival…
She trained as a runner –
you wouldn't have a chance.

Tonight you're shut out from the beach-house.
Storms roll up the bay.
Even with curtains drawn, lights out
and your back to the wall, you're not
anonymous enough to be safe.

II

Sheltered behind a cliff
where only rugged plants dig in,
grass hair on the roof streams back.

On a calm day you like to sit up there,
drawn to horizon and cloudscape,
roaming the whitecaps, sucking the wind

Or in the evening face the other way
contemplate the garden
and the shady plain behind it
utterly devoid of folk, their sheep, and all their striving.

Rock is your friend:
nobody builds here,
nobody farms on scrubby sand
a day's walk from anywhere.

This is a place of healing:
of sleep and recollection.
No mirrors in this tiny room
carved from the bank –
just everything you need.

Shepherd

He stands in the doorway
to keep it open
I can't see anything
for white light

I would step past him
eyes straight ahead
if I wanted to get in
and he was blind

So

So
what more?
And would you really?

Think!
It is already
round and enough.

Earthly Paradise
in two moves –
except

Pain.
Where is it:
No? Or no power?

No's hard is
finalfinalfinal
Cop that.

No power is
mirror mirror
shallow to infinity.

Life is shapeless,
an old coat.
Wear it.

No Possums

there are no possums in heaven
no leaf curl or black spot
nectarines are perfect
the robinia's whole

there are no birds in heaven
no silver-eye or greenfinch
no least sparrow
spore or seed

there are no flowers in heaven
no show-off lotus
or multifoliate rose
the fruit is all

the fruit is perfect
without any seed
the sky is endless
inimitable blue

Portrait of a Religious Man

Eyebrows raised with eyes closed
face tilted to   what

almost smiling as if to
Go on it's as you

But it's also a flinch sustained
as if to   it's been so

of course you
I'd be glad but for more

most of all it's
not saying

a come-on
held
    open

After Long Darkness

My eyes flick down and sideways
in your familiar gesture
when doing thought in public.
Birds are singing their heads off.

I'm about to look up when I know
just what I'll see when I do:
a table's perimeter
pleasant with tea things,

a walled garden
straight out of Cambridge,
foliage reflecting
your eyes' green-and-blue.

Thirty-two years! I'll say
as I refill your cup,
relieved to be here at last
drinking tea with you.

Aphasia, Exile, Outlawry

I

One of those nights. You and sleep playing tag,
though only one of you thinks it's a game. I *will*
rest, you say, I *will* go home: I just
need to find the words from the water garden.

You haul them up from the well, but they smear like ink.
They belong to your real life that you abandoned:
there where the wattles bloom and corn and 'taters grow.
Eucalypsis, apocalypsis…
Every night you make a run for home.

In exile language fades away, unused,
till the whole tree languishes.
Words are comfortless as bare boards;
you pace about forgetting what you came for,
till some new nick or syllable
        stumps your softened feet
        and thrills you to the quick.

You have to believe the long-sought words will come
like Bo-peep's proverbials safely grazing
a suburban garden full of virtual magpies:
plumbago
        frangipani
                Hardenbergia

II

All photos lie. But something's caught
in this one: faster than a speeding bullet,
a flying blur in tabard and trousers,
if you're caught, it's
        waiting and preparing and serving.
left alone you
        climb trees and run fast and sing,
        pledge fealty to the forest and the life of an outlaw.

Peep peep peep cry all the little girls
from the West Indies, Americky and Spain.
We're nearly three and a whizz at words
on which we know the universe depends.
We repeat: we hear you loud and clear.
We're pretty sure you can't hear us at all.

        Maid Marianne's maids are we.
        If you call, we are not at home.
        We're dining very publicly
        With the Sheriff of Nottingham.

        The Sheriff has a fulsome set.
        His words line up without a gap.
        He'd sentence us without a second thought.
        It's just as well he cannot hear our hearts.

Peep peep peep, all the women cry
In Ireland and Australia and France.
It's just as well he cannot read our smile:
Our voices are inviolate and clear.

III

This table's had hard use. The grain
is coming through in tiny elevations.
I run my fingers lightly up and down,
learning the long contours. And I know
something about how my life has gone.

This evening I've been marking papers
on the colonised and their oppressors,
their strategies my strategies,
fully theorised – and on my shelf,
lest I forget.

You know what happens to outlaws. Such is life.
So don that pencil skirt, sharpen your nose,
powder the old perruque. And remember,
you can never be lost, knowing
home is any place where poems are.

Exile

Double Vision

I

At thirty-three thousand feet
gold glinting jigsaw pieces: lakes
nestled everywhere in deepest green.
Quebec: antithetical landscape.
Tilting westward now. What on earth
is that colour of the sky?
I remove dark glasses, strain
at the port-hole's double glazing.
I'm flying into colour with no name –
stubborn,
        stubborn,
as an eggshell-blue horizon
where cloud shapes reflect exactly
the puff of eucalypts.

II

So the bus has a tilt-back seat,
the foot-bar the plane lacked,
a restroom equipped for my convenience –
Don't gawk around.
Relax, admire the trees
revealing fabled splendour
bough by leisured bough.
Remember, it's not money
growing on that rich soil.

III

On the way from the airport
no one was more joyful or self-mocking
or ready for a North American miracle
in that Greyhound coach mythy with Kerouac,
goggling yet half-smiling like Madame Merle
at my largest block of flats so far.
'But no, they're really *apartments*.' (I'd not yet
heard of *condominiums*.)
We turned, entered a tunnel dark with oil and spittle –
Then – (Dear God! What is it!)
Civic, vast, full frontal,
The Royal York Hotel,
with gleaming verticals of gold and copper
of all the banks in full choir:
apotheosis of commerce at sunset.

IV

Seen from Ward Island
the city's geometry
sharp as a postcard.

V

Just
shutting the door behind you:
> the brittle air, a wad of snow
> and the street, the city
forever foreign –
But dogs are everywhere and everywhere
cheering, and this one is frisky
as he trots over to the pole. Then hesitates…
and lifts a leg, as obvious as cliché.

VI

Pleasure and fear of forgetting:
two sides of a coin,
the soundless anarchy of falling snow
separating you from recognition.
You have to get around on memory.

So you're always alert in the streetcar
trying to think past the whited double glazing.
Toronto, Toronto,
how does your mesh of street names go?
– tracing the lost night outside.

But wandering around sleep,
my mind turns to your stoic gardens
linked beyond their chains in whiteness.

Summer Song, Toronto

Three nights of solid heat have brought me here
to this, my cool nest on the balcony
slung from the side of the house like a pannier
holding rain scent, bird cry.

My privilege, to keep the last defence
of these sleeping hours, or contemplate
the alternations of indifference
and mystery, in the breeze swinging the gate.

A whisper comes from nowhere, soft mirage…
A streetlight catches the sibilance of a thigh…
There's a man there, muttering, pacing his roof like a stage,
goaded by heat into soliloquy.

A pregnant moment. He walks right to the edge –
and stands there, elbows folded, looking out.
At length he murmurs something I can't catch –
And turns, and goes back to his window, and through into heat.

I shall keep my glasses on tonight, that the stars,
so strangely choired, may send their influence:
after so many eons of light, to miss the last
tiny revelation by an inch…

From a Tall Building in Toronto

Spruces are always pointerly:
a stand of cardboard 'A's propped for a Northern scene.
Next, a row of houses, fixed as rock:
steep gables zigzagged with snow,
or that one with its point shorn off
like a Dutch headdress
perched on stolid brick:
a street of jam jars with paper lids.
A city of details, of fragments,
of adjectives cleaving like snow.

Red brick and black wooden ledge,
roof slate and chimney and the no-colour tips of bare tree:
each thing perfectly laden,
each delicate highlight,
a sweetness held,
        almost suppliant,
                in its separate clarity.

But the whole remains elusive: glittering fruits
refuse arrangement, shape no constellation
for the eye, no view.
Daubed everywhere with white
that does not fade with distance:
a city spread flat to the sky.

So you must make a virtue out of movement,
though your eye jabs like a grackle's beak,
or Io pursued by a blackfly.

> *Go subtly as a stream of ink*
> *through the papery air.*
> *Weave like a serpent,*
> *dance in your task, thread*
> *image after scale-bright image…*
>
> *Only leave in your train*
> *loop upon loop of memory,*
> *a pathway, a pattern of going.*

Doubt

Cede it no weight –
then comes the huge coil barrelling over.
This is doubt, harmless as thunder.

How hollowness resounds!
my dearest hours squandered –
love whimsically declined –

How clear is that spring!
How pellucid predestiny!
My body lasts and lasts.

Letter in December

Light without shadow: snow light,
opaque to the point of reflectiveness –
like the envelope in my hand.
A voice is speaking softly,
reedily, perfectly modulated,
with its slightest lisp still catching the corners…
Suddenly I'm smiling at a chair,
as if recognition's alchemy of sparks
arced through the air between us.
I almost saw you blink, too,
as if you, too, were still a bit dazzled.

In Melbourne there's a heatwave:
yesterday was a scorcher: forty-one;
and you're still knocking it back on weekends,
and working for the paper,
and I see you've learned their computer:
your letter's in dot matrix.

Has this been filed? Am I part of a larger audience?
I hear your sudden, teasing laughter:
a happy cynic reassuring no one.
It's snowing here, in case you were wondering.

> *Fine grains of snow clouding the page…*
> *footsteps snapping in the brittle air…*
> *a muted city yielding up its distances…*
> *the land contracting till it crushes its own bones…*

It seems that all codes, too, break
of themselves in the end, as every letter here
is riddled with emptiness that is full of meaning.
I listen as your voice crumbles in white noise,
the tiny repeated tappings of a fingernail,
then the sound of falling snow.

London

a leaden sound,
convergence of streets and meaning,
clumped and insoluble,
like a fist in the pit of your stomach.

Something gets under your fingernails,
clots at the roots of your hair,
like spittle and tar congealed on the pavement,
plaster grotesqueries crusted in terminal grime.

It's all finished, it's history:
the sheer monuments of will,
testaments of civic desire,
all completed public projects,
eon upon eon, as far as you can see.
Deep in your bones you know
the whole thing's built on rubbish.

But you continue, always in shadow,
to walk between walls,
cling to the clefts between heights.
Always in shadow,
the body continues to contract, as with cold,
and the mind is released from form.
So you breathe in the shallow rustications of brick,
crouch behind gargoyles,
thieve what you can,
though iron bars bulb the windows of your eyes
and doors deadbolt like gunshot.

No one gathers fuel in vacant lots.
You can't burn that stuff at home.
It's against the law, and anyway,
it won't catch.

Morning Song

Break of day:
an Arctic wind
howls down Eccleston Square

And Ruth on the balcony
spry as a child
combing her long white hair.

After the Great Storm

Well, I thought, that was a
strong wind last night.
And I said, it's only fear, only
fear, because of the ocean between us.

But from the morning window:
the moss-encrusted corner wall
smashed to gravel;
almost all the branches gone
from the pointy spruce;
the whole mountain ash stretched out,
like a long thigh,
towards the single mothers' home,
its leaves brushing the windows.

And apples, apples everywhere
flinging their rounded reds,
and small birds flitting
among the grounded branches.

Colchester, a walking song

Lao-tzu said,
Where soldiers are garrisoned
brambles and thorns will grow –
like these waist-high bleached stalks,
stiff as beeswax in late summer light.
Fulsome as that light,
as this silence
between bursts of Sunday
firecrackers or rifle shot.

In this garrison town of two thousand years
Roman bones persist beneath
the Essex County Hospital,
where gross Victorian patriarchs
plied their knives and chisels.
The names of centurions last, inscribed in stone;
the names of the criminals used for medical experiments
are relics of paper and their bodies dispersed.

Where soldiers are garrisoned brambles grow
and are gathered by women
hoping to remain unknown –
whose names are snagged
in the parchments of St Osyth's hanging judge.

Soldiers destroy evidence of their destinies;
there are no maps of Northern Ireland here.
They go, leaving the ripped pages,
to a featureless place, illegible
as the contours of a desert.

On Hilly Fields the brambles spread unchecked
where Thomas Fairfax and his men laid siege
to the walled town. When night brought respite from
the cannon and the musket fire, by moonlight,
he pored over every patient street.

In six months gorse and blackberry covered the slain;
now blood-bright hawthorn berries prove the ground.
In the slanted light of the dying year
we follow the foxes' path into a clearing
and stop. A big rabbit,
deaf as his gun-deafened ancestors,
sits with its back to us, snuffing the air.

Radio Drama

Repeats
like plate glass
lock out the world.
You get to anticipating
Clarrie's next line,
anaesthetised in the middle of the day
while the west wind slams against the house
and apples bruise in the bowl.
Elsewhere,
behind the radio's mask –
its illusion of repeatable time –
the heartbeat batters on;
stations you're not listening to
catch the people's cries.

In Memoriam Francis Barker

There was never a man sat stiller,
           all in black and ankle crooked on knee,
never a man whose silence
           compelled us more to thought and questioning
Dark lodestone
whose every effort availed him not a tittle
in his battle with his calling.
Latter-day divine,
intriguing as a riddle.

A bloody blade of a mind, yet patient:
teaching us the computer, listening to our half-
formed questions, explaining deconstruction
in words like slow fuses, standing at the lectern
to denounce the idea of a
university totting up success in bricks and books
till the managerial sentences of the anniversary prospectus
toppled at the touch of his voice,
and ours, in ravelled laughter.

I have kept these lessons by me nine years now,
weapons or gifts to hold
that tremulous place where the
tongue falters and the throat constricts –

Gathered together at the edge of the year,
too soon too late this dismal morning,
we stand up straighter to be counted.

Poem in April

(for Bob)

Chill and warmth and chill,
remorseless as fever the season assails us.
Blasted beyond thought,
we cringe as we awaken.

Yesterday, I planted a fuchsia,
fragrant earth warming my hand;
today pulses of snow and freezing rain,
in counterpoint or at crossed purposes,

sculpt huge forms that linger in air:
monumental giants search the streets,
or turn toward each other
as in the depths of sleep.

Dreams merge and part
as easily as cloud,
beads of a story
tremble on the skin:

points along a fault line that divides us
more than the salt Atlantic.

Tatton Park

(In memory of Martyn Edwards)

Just for a few moments there
the background music for the promotion of sanity
quiets – we must have left it in the car –
And, briefly,
we are four animals
leaning out into pearl brittle with cold.
The dry slats of the jetty
barely sustain us, yet they do
and here we are
for a few minutes
amongst these gracile animals
half small-boned cow, half tree,
cropping peacefully in the unearthly
smoke-blue mist
of an ice-cold afternoon.

Song for Esther

Woman far walking
flying and walking
came north to sing

found
horizontal rain
forty-five-degree rain
rain sliding off stone
seeping through rough brick

a shallow-puddled land
unmoving underfoot
no giant mother turning in her sleep
no mother tongue

no water plashing
over rocky hills
sinking into earth
no rainbow valley weaving dreams

Like her namesake Esther walked
the paved streets, a foreign queen –
farthest flying
woman warrior:
Esther,
sole Maori in Manchester,
singing her song

Notes from the First Gulf War

I The Taking of POWs, 26/2/91

Out of the
        grave-deep
                clamp-shaped trench
they stand.
They stand up
out of their grave
and in the painful light
are not shot.
The paunchy ones tell them to kneel
        they kneel they plead
        too scared to grasp assurances
        but anything anything

They lie prone in the sand
while enemies-turned-mercymen
probe with machine-guns.
Then one by one they strip and kneel
in pitiless light.
Only when humiliation is certain
does a man
turn to face the legions of the defeated;
thousands and thousands of them
in a line stretching out of sight.

II In Essex County Hospital

In the middle of the night
        two beds along
                cried out.
A nurse hurried over.
        'He can't get in here, can he?'
                (sobbing with terror).
Six eyelids flickered
        on drug-closed eye-holes;
                we knew whom she meant.)

III QF2 MEL–LHR, 20/2/91

In the dark capsule
thirty-seven thousand feet up
we struggle from sleep:
another surprising amenity –
ITN news of the War to our left, just
beyond the faint grey skyline.

In a costume sponsored by World War II
in pillar-box jacket and round
white clip-on earrings,
a woman with diction so pure
hair so smooth
the studio lights make a halo,
speaks of 'a long and distinguished tradition'
of war.
We watch
through image intensifier
the beads of white light rise;
we hear through head-sets
that ten thousand people perish each day –
such round numbers, absolute zeros,
magnify our stupefaction.

Somewhat to our dismay,
we find we really believe
the plastic-lipped woman's a fiction;
only the faintest painted sneer
betrays the animal origin of her words.
Suddenly, with stunning obviousness,
a real baby –
in a cradle clipped to the wall beneath the movie screen –
wakes, screaming louder than the sound-track.
And his mother picks him up
and rocks him
standing there in front of the picture,
tattooed by the news story,
thirty-seven thousand feet up
– in the future's lead light.

IV Desert Fires, Viewed from a Plane

They used to be so comforting:
those plumes of flame,
                        fire spume,
flaring hugely in the dark –

that is, the otherwise dark, unmakeoutable
depths,
witnesses to a vigil:
endurance of sheer distance
when all around me slept –

Then, I was grateful for those
false signs of habitation –
those telltale fire foundations
hiding daylight scenes perhaps of desolation.
Before we were declared enemies in war,
these were my talismans against the dark.

So, too, in England,
trying to imagine the glance of the foe,
I am sad, watching
the giant copper beech
like a lion's head
freeze to a mere sign,
heraldic and inimical.

Moorings

Moonrise (a fragment)

Halfway up the wall,
the framed hole in the light
hangs square and still –
a photograph   of house tops   beckoning

to the gardens, where giant
elms hover
like dreams at anchor –
grey, volcanic, puffed-out memories
of spurting stone.
Their peaks are pale against the sky.
No wind moves them.

> Standing on the sill,
> toes, knuckles, elbows, all
> angle to grip.

Then, shuddering
galvanised iron under your feet; brick
pressing in your shoulder blades.
You crouch there like a gargoyle
in the cold wind. Hair streams like wild grass
from a face of stone.
This brave blankness, this vigil.

The house was called The Moorings

The house was called The Moorings. In creeper-covered
solitude, between river curve and road curve,
it might have been a mansion. Once,
far back behind its stiffening face,
a delicate pattern of fungus confusing the mouldings
unfurled in rich ochre of nicotine
as Mr Forsythe, deaf and on crutches, struck
heavily across the floor.
At night: the house steeped in earth-chill;
a merciless grandfather clock…
The daughter, Jean, was lithe and vigorous.
Her hair sprang out in golden waves like a princess's;
her musician's hands were deft
in the black-and-white laundry.
I knew we were close to the river: all through the wash-cycle
I watched water shadow on the ceiling
and sang 'Jimmy Walen'.

In my absence   dry leaves fell like a veil
from painted prongs
deep wet clay clove to sheer steel
stone was crushed and dispersed
talk of compensation
completed an absence

Riverlight breathed though the rooms,
reflecting every surface like an echo.
Outside it settled, thick as hair,
on an acre of grass, perfect for handstands,
twined around a monkeybars-for-three
where I played supple as water.
When the gong rang for dinner
I was springing in a rainbow
across the buoyant turf,
blinded by the house shadow at sunset.

>
> Face in the cabinet mirror
> swings open,
> mauve walls and green linoleum
> fold in like a flower,
> she bent
>   from her height
>   the Golden Fleece

In an after-ether haze
I heard them speak of a fall, live coals,
the night grown brisk and silent.
I looked at my arm: saw skin
shrivelled like hibiscus – a taut
shining pool
        an oval watermark
                riverlight tattoo

Knee to knee we talk and laugh,
lean forward as if
into the wind. Behind your words
the tyres make a sound like rain
our profiles wax and wane
the freeway curves for no reason

and the curve seems longer, endless – somewhere here
must be a buried house, a riverbed.
Water-smooth skin lies numb under material. We talk
above the constant painless abrasion of tyre on road.

This is a false memory

This is a false memory
you never said anything you were only
looking at a photo of me
with sun on my hair

You are facing into the dark
you say
with the smugness of those who've turned round

Rejection

Rejection. And
after the rite of tears,
silence.

I lie helpless in the bedclothes.
The night deepens. The clock ticks.
One bird sings, 'My life, my life, my life…'

But silence remains at the back of things.
It does not push or call.
It is the place where songs are gathered
and laid down as burdens

as of a shelf above the shards
of anger, grief: the heap of memories.
At the heart of the swirling night music
it remains whole as porcelain.

Poem for Caro

Almost by agreement, begin with
your hair – the long nostalgic current
in which I too am mingled,
and then to coax out of its darkness
your ivory profile
intent on the sudden flame:
> but what words could
> shine for you, vibrate to your name,
> your slow voice, your body's
> soft blunted shapes?

Return to an open room:
endless drove of trucks grinds three feet from the glass,
electric slur of voices shatters space behind that wall,
but here
is calm air.
Not one room but eight.
You build your homes on the sheer
edge of the city. Bed, chair, mirror, books rest
solid as icons here.
> (In a different doorway
> your hands buried in your sleeves
> unsure, as yet, how gentlest to pry me
> from the stillborn poem.)

Once, in the snow, in a dream
having arrived before the appointed hour
I passed the time in scanning the horizon
the sky dense as black paper
until you were there, your face
bright with its own colour
as we strolled past familiar invisible streets
under the bell's greeting
our voices converging –
then darkness like water rising, I was falling,
                                dying,
                                          calling your name.

There is always a hinge in a nightmare –
        some trick in the voice, some failure of trust:
        the inevitable corpse
        shrivels in the undergrowth

so when you spoke –
troubled, slow –
I was saved and knew it
borne upward into waking.

All night, the wind warm as breath
a curtain lifting, falling
tired phrases turning like leaves
the city lying
like a secret between us.

Nocturne

Pen scratch. Breath ebbs and flows.
What sound
could pull you back so
sharply into too much light?
Only floorboard: footstep.

But what is that small second sound
behind, inside the other? Faint rub,
perhaps, of metal on metal…crystallising
        recognising
                coins shifting with the weight in a boot

I stare at the door, knowing
that the hand reaching to turn my mind
was always yours, yours the half-face
at night, the knuckles round the railing,
the car door opening –
this house was built against you, silent one.

Enough. I cough.
I close my pen with a click.
I take up my brush, quickly avoiding
eyes in the mirror.
Now smooth the sheets and soothe yourself with thought…
Humour is the anodyne:
before you turn the light off
scan the walls for spiders.

Sans Bulot

The bench's fixed gaze; tendrils of ivy
quavering between iron spikes;
random, futile, your thoughts
pulsing like rain

and some days the street – the whole hill – lifts
under you, and you rail against the city
refusing your entry, refusing your birthright,
refusing your anger – till your image returns
(slowly, as through water) and you are
awkward: an amphibian kicking
bitterly against thin air.

Afterwards, for hours, quietly drawing back
from the exhausted city…
One cold afternoon, you'll see it
resting on the turning earth.

Mother

In the mirror my watched face
always stiffens to repose.
Item: two eyebrows, arched for emphasis;
item: two eyes, semicircular –
Esserman heirlooms
muted in successive generations;
item: thick, dark hair – mine longer, massy –
yours cut and set. When
I stroke your forehead,
you smile, relieved by my hand's night coldness.

Choking with nostalgia now,
I follow you down the ticking hall,
your silhouette in the yellow light
walking   a little stiffly
with a separate knowledge –
one might learn complete service by thus rehearsing –
but the mind, the mind's leap to agony
while you tell yourself all night that the way is
through terror not around it –
striving for those long, mesmerising paradoxes
to lull under control not
death but these spasms of fear –

Mother, mortal ignorance is
your betrayed eyes,
all my tender gestures
wither in my arms.

Task (Visiting Grandpa)

You will need
a cigarette before starting the car, and one
in Punt Road, and one to guide you safely through the
car park, hardy native garden,
brick path, automatic door, ah,
SMOKERS PLEASE
You'll watch the protean glow worm counting the floors;
you'll avoid the eye of the Queen, billowing like a galleon,
sitting sidesaddle,
and the rich aftertaste of nicotine will drown
in the smell like a bucket of lavender.

How often does he see
tall willows and poplars behind
two sets of glass doors?
What can the mirror show him in his bed?
Who gave him this commission
that fumbles each slow word
to measure the King's locks?
Now, panicky, suspecting amnesia,
he gropes for the name of the man who designed the device
his hand clamped to the pair of bone tongs
he had at the lab.
Still the faithful servant of the State:
he tells me the King's locks,
once measured,
can never be stolen.

>   His whole will holding
>   to the precious vestiges…

Last week: liquid fear
streaming down his face:
some well-meaning nurse,
sympathising with problems of measurement,
encouraged him
to calculate his age.

Intimations

Always,
on the other side of my eye –
a black hole
my child mind thought was my soul.
One hole or two. Tunnels.
The long hours passed in simple speculation –
but in nightmare everything dilated as the
serpent from the pantomime rippled up the corridor to
bite me awake.

And the other was just as distressing:
(my father confused in pyjamas –)
'But Daddy! Can't you see the dots?'
I could hardly see him
for tiny plosive red-and-blue pied wings

They still fly, indelible,
tracing all night their slow curve
eastward.

Four a.m.

Thick, moist air. Any minute now
wind will bring back the streets, colour
will seep into the sky, the room.
Meanwhile after-images of sleep
sail lordly by,
faces blandly folding closed
exude a thousand little sighs,
a corner of the curtain lifts,
there remain two lidless eyes.

Thoughts shaken in their matchbox.
Dud thoughts, dud words, no weaponry.
And the eyes narrow with certainty and the brain
beating its denial at the skull's brittle wall
                             a hairsbreadth
                                       dissolving

And then a memory
(a shadow unfolding from the corner): it is the body.
Prickle of skin. Dots of cold light.
It is the body
that remembers, that brings in
melody inevitable while the world drags
home across the fault line.
Words somersaulting into meaning pattern a question:
whether to regret that instant's passing –
the brain's utter daring
when the body flickers and grows dark...
On my hands, on my forehead, where
dark hair cradles the bone –
full beads of sweat.
In the grey aftermath I am brimming with mercy.

www.ingramcontent.com/pod-product-compliance
Lightning Source LLC
Chambersburg PA
CBHW062143100526
44589CB00014B/1674